Ultimate Beginner Tech Start Series
MIDI Basics

C000002462

By Lee Whitmore

WARNER BROS. PUBLICATIONS - THE GLOBAL LEADER IN PRINT
USA: 15800 NW 48th Avenue, Miami, FL 33014

WARNER/CHAPPELL MUSIC

CANADA: 40 SHEPPARD AVE. WEST, SUITE 800
TORONTO, ONTARIO, M2N 6K9
SCANDINAVIA: P.O. BOX 533, VENDEVAGEN 85 B
S-182 15, DANDERYD, SWEDEN
AUSTRALIA: P.O. BOX 353
3 TALAVERA ROAD, NORTH RYDE N.S.W. 2113

NUOVA CARISCH

ITALY: VIA CAMPANIA, 12
20098 S. GIULIANO MILANESE (MI)
ZONA INDUSTRIALE SESTO ULTERIANO
SPAIN: MAGALLANES, 25
28015 MADRID
FRANCE: 20, RUE DE LA VILLE-L'EVEQUE, 75008 PARIS

INTERNATIONAL MUSIC PUBLICATIONS LIMITED

ENGLAND: GRIFFIN HOUSE,
161 HAMMERSMITH ROAD, LONDON W6 8BS
GERMANY: MARSTALLSTR. 8, D-80539 MUNCHEN
DENMARK: DANMUSIK, VOGNMAGERGADE 7
DK 1120 KOBENHAVNK

Editor: Debbie Cavalier
Cover Design: Debbie Johns Lipton
Layout: Debbie Johns Lipton
Character Illustration: Ken Rehm

Acknowledgments

Thanks to Stoney Stockell for telling stories; to Elvin Rodriguez, Robert Corley and Stanley Bednarz for "reading it once and checking it twice"; and to editor Debbie Cavalier for the opportunity and support. Special appreciation to Laura Whitmore for preparing diagrams, reading, and, as always, being there.

Contents

Chapter One

What Is MIDI?

MIDI. [midi] [mee - dee] [my - dy] [mid - ee]

Which pronunciation is it? What is it? What is it for? What does it do?

Is it a box? Some very technical, high-end piece of gear? Where do I plug it in? Do I have to have one? Will I find it on the Internet? Do I have to be a master programmer or maestro to use it — master it?

These are just some of the questions that arise when folks first become acquainted with MIDI (actually pronounced, mi - dee). No doubt, something like the following has happened to you (before I got into computer music I had a similar experience).

You visit a friend who has a home studio. An amateur guitar player and computer music hobby-ist, he has a handful of gear, including a computer with a sound card, an electronic keyboard, a multitrack recorder, and a couple of effects boxes. As you talk, your friend, itching to show off his latest stuff, cranks up his PC, turns on his mixer and powered monitors. He starts his computer music recording program, presses PLAY, and voila!

It sounds great, and you can't believe that he pulled it off. You know he has a little music back-ground, but this is amazing. You hear drums, bass, guitar, and some horns. Wow! It is really impressive, and you congratulate your friend. Modest as he is, he shrugs it off and says, "It was nothing." It sounds like a lot more than just a little "nothing" to you, and you return with, "You have got to be kidding! That must have taken weeks to put together." Your friend says, "That's not even mine — it is a song file I downloaded from the Internet. I simply opened the file in my computer's MIDI song player, and pressed START. All it takes is MIDI. Now let me play you one of my originals."

Your friend is being more than a little nonchalant. It can't really be that easy. He tells you all you need is a computer and a sound generator, like a synthesizer or sound card in your PC, and you can get started. If you want to create your own tunes, then you have to have some kind of MIDI-capable electronic musical instrument.

You have a computer at home, and walk into your local music store the next day to verify just how far your friend was pulling your leg. You walk over to the computer music area of the store and see a wall of gear. Looks pretty intimidating, to say the least. The keyboard/computer salesper-son introduces herself, asks you how you are, and then starts "fishing." "What gear do you have at home? What are you looking to do? Are you a producer? Have a home studio?" You reply, "I am not a producer, so slow down. I have a new PC, just saw a friend, who I thought knew nothing about composing or playing electronic music, and he blew me away by playing a bunch of tunes that he downloaded from the Internet. I have the same type of machine, and wanted to see if it really is as easy as he says. He told me all I need is MIDI."

Now you are in trouble. The salesperson lights up, and launches into a litany of the latest and the greatest. She tells you, "Yeah, you have a good PC, but, you have to have this interface, that software program, this keyboard," and on and on.

Is it really that complicated? Do you really need all of that stuff? Her high-end description makes it sound like MIDI is something that should be relegated to the elite of computer programmers and technogeek musicians — the guys who sit in their studios 24 hours a day staring at their 17-inch monitors, drooling over line after line of computer code in an event list.

It is not that complicated. In fact, MIDI is a simple thing. It was created to make things simple. If you have any computer, Mac or PC, and have some kind of sound generating device, you can make music with MIDI. Or, if you have an electronic keyboard workstation that has a multitrack recorder (called a sequencer) inside, you can also make music without a computer. Most synthesizers, keyboards, and other self-contained music workstations already have MIDI capability built-in. If you have a Windows-based PC with a sound card you are ready to play MIDI tunes now. If you have an Apple computer and can get on the Internet, all you need to get started is some software called QuickTime. QuickTime has a software-synthesizer built-in, and enables your computer to play tunes with MIDI. No other gear is required.

So What Is It — Really?

MIDI is an acronym that stands for: "Musical Instrument Digital Interface." It is what it says. Think about it. The key is the word interface. If you look up that word the dictionary will tell you that "interface" is both a noun and a verb. Both definitions shed light on what MIDI is:

1. As a verb, to "interface" is to work cooperatively, or to come together. For instance, say you work in accounting at your job. Your boss tells you to help prepare the year-end report for the executives. Can you write the report yourself? No. You have to work with other departments, like marketing, sales, distribution, etc. In order to get a clear picture of the company, where it is, and how it works, you have to work with other people who have their own areas of expertise. By working with these other people, you "interface" with other departments, translating the information you have into words and concepts that are meaningful to them, while asking them to do the same for you.

2. As a noun, an "interface" is a device that allows two or more pieces of equipment to communicate. A specialized piece of hardware and/or software, it allows two different devices, like two electronic musical instruments, or an electronic musical instrument and a computer, for example, to talk to each other and to work together.

Do you see the similarities between these things? The connection between the noun and verb makes a good analogy to MIDI and its components (hardware and software). The noun and verb have something in common — they refer to making things or people work together — and that is what MIDI does. It is an interface, hardware and software that allows different devices, like musical instruments and computers to work together.

MIDI consists of many things, but in its entirety, it is a "standard," or specification. Broken down into its component parts, MIDI is several things, including a hardware standard, a software standard, a standard set of sounds, and more. In comparison to today's rapid advance in computers and networks, it is an "old" technology. Conceived in the eighties, and agreed upon and implemented in 1984, MIDI has become an enduring and guiding force in the development and application of music technology.

Computer companies, instrument manufacturers, publishers, composers, arrangers and hobbyists all use MIDI. Hardware companies and engineers think about it a lot in the design and creation of instruments, and in making software that makes these instruments run. On the other hand, musicians, multimedia designers and home computer users, who also use MIDI often, rarely think about it — and that is the point. MIDI is supposed to make using different music and technology devices easy. So unless you are designing devices that use MIDI, you shouldn't have to think about it very often.

Chapter Two

A Little History

MIDI is a standard, created in cooperation by members of the music industry, mostly hardware manufacturers and some publishers and computer folks. It makes computers, electronic keyboards and synthesizers, other MIDI controllers, electronic music accessories and software easy to use together. It should simply be there, running in the "background" as you play, compose and make electronic music.

Now that we have a conceptual definition of MIDI, let's investigate why MIDI came about. Its origins lend a lot to mastering ways to use MIDI. Here is a little electronic music history to lend perspective. It is time to step into the "Virtual MIDI Museum" and look at a couple of exhibits that will help us understand how to use MIDI.

EXHIBIT 1:
The first exhibit in the museum is a display of old instruments. In it sit the famous and classic synthesizers that keyboard players drool over. These are the instruments that got it all started, from the Moog to the Arp to that huge, early synthesizer from the Columbia-Princeton University studios in New Jersey. The earliest synthesizers took up enough floor space to fill an exhibit hall in the Smithsonian. They were huge supercomputers that did nothing more than play one note at a time!

Figure 2.1 Moog Synthesizer

The Columbia-Princeton instrument and other early sound development machines were created in the seventies. In a short period of time, electronic components became smaller and smaller, and cheaper and cheaper, allowing innovators like Bob Moog to create portable electronic synthesizers that were small enough to be carried from place to place. By the mid-seventies, it was commonplace to see an armory of synthesizers covering the stage of the classic rock and roll bands, like the Moody Blues; Emerson, Lake and Palmer; and Yes.

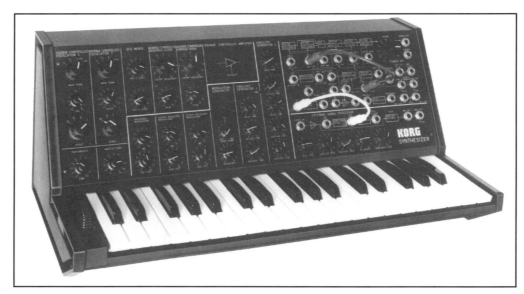

Figure 2.2 Korg MS20

The earliest synthesizers were monophonic and monotimbral. Sound like gibberish? These are high-tech terms that are really very simple. "Monophonic" means that these early instruments could play just one note at a time. "Monotimbral" means that these instruments could play only one timbre, or tone color, at a time. For example, all of the first early synthesizers could sound one note, or key, at a time. That one note sounded like a single instrument, i.e., like one note played on a trumpet, or one note played on a piano or a guitar.

This is a very basic, elementary concept, but it is important, Think about it. The first synthesizers were big, bulky and expensive in today's terms, and could play only one note at a time. That note sounded like a single instrument, and took lots of time to set up. If you were playing and wanted to change to a contrasting timbre, say from a trumpet sound to a guitar sound, it was a lot of work. You had to start pulling and repatching cables, and it took a lot of skill and knowledge of the concepts of synthesis and the operation of the synthesizer to make it happen.

Today, if you want to change from one sound to another on your keyboard, you press a switch, or punch in a number. Today's instruments have hundreds of sounds built-in, and you can play back many (usually up to sixteen) simultaneously — that is enough to reproduce a combo or medium-sized orchestra — all from one electronic instrument!

The number of sounds and number of timbres available in early instruments were a driving force behind why MIDI was created. The early synthesizer manufacturers knew that players would quickly tire of their monophonic, monotimbral synthesizers, and would want to replicate ensembles with more complex orchestrations — more instruments at one time. They also knew that if they were able to combine, or layer, the best sounds from two of their instruments at the same time, controlled from one synthesizer, that they could create very attractive and appealing sounds for players.

In a nutshell, that was one of the main reasons why MIDI was created. And it encouraged synthesizer manufacturers to work together. The need was to create an "interface," a standard way to connect two electronic keyboards together, and let them communicate in order to work in tandem.

EXHIBIT 2:
The second exhibit in the Virtual MIDI Museum has a big plaque over it with the year "1983." This is where it (MIDI) all began. This exhibit is filled with pictures of the innovators who conceived MIDI and its precursors, framed documents with the MIDI specification, and the first few MIDI instruments (on pedestals, of course).

MIDI was originally conceived by electronic music and synthesis pioneer Dave Smith, who was the head, and founder, of a company called Sequential Circuits in the early 1980s. Dave presented a paper at the international meeting of the Audio Engineering Society in 1981.

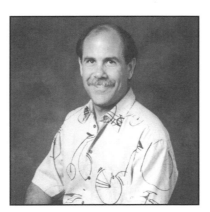

Figure 2.3 Dave Smith

At the time he gave the paper in New York, in October of that year, MIDI was just a glimmer in his eye. Just the same, the essential concept of what it was to become was there. He proposed a standard connection, or interface, that would allow different manufacturers' synthesizers to control each other. In other words, he hoped that by connecting two synthesizer keyboards together with something like a standard guitar patch cable, one could control the other.

From that meeting and presentation, a small group of music industry people, and some electronic musicians, left, thought about the idea, and kept the flame alive. Eventually, in January of 1982, a larger group of industry representatives got together to discuss the idea once again at the NAMM show (meeting of the National Association of Music Merchants). A few key components of MIDI were agreed upon, and the group went its separate ways, with an assignment — to create the original specification, or guidelines, for MIDI — a standardized "Musical Instrument Digital Interface."

There were some big twists in the road ahead as MIDI was being planned and the original version of the specification authored. For instance, one of the first MIDI instruments, Yamaha's DX7, was introduced after the NAMM meeting, but before the MIDI specification was completed. This instrument became one of the best-selling instruments of all time, and the first huge commercially successful MIDI-capable electronic keyboard. Regretfully, it was released before the MIDI specification was completed and agreed upon, and had many misimplemented MIDI functions.

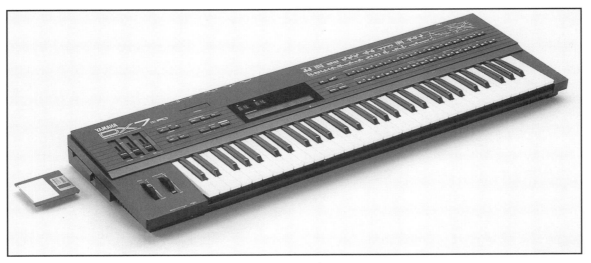

Figure 2.4 Yamaha DX7

Yamaha wasn't the only company to rush to the gate and try to implement MIDI first, and all who jumped on the idea early implemented some strange variations on what was to become the first MIDI specification. Because technology is always evolving, it was, and has always been difficult to keep MIDI current with innovations in technology and musical equipment.

The skeleton of what MIDI was to become started to take shape. In the following decade, in addition to defining how one instrument could communicate with and control another, MIDI also has come to embody things like:

- **Time Code:** a standard that allows electronic musical instruments to stay synchronized with other studio audio equipment.
- **Machine Control:** a standard that allows electronic musical instruments and other recording studio-related devices, like tape decks and video players and recorders, to be controlled and work together.
- **Show Control:** a standard that allows devices on stage, like lights and set components, to work together during a performance.
- **General MIDI:** a standard set of instrument sounds shared by electronic musical instruments and computers alike.
- **Standard MIDI Files:** a standard file-format for sharing and exchanging MIDI recordings, or sequences, between different hardware and software tools.
- **Sound Files:** a standard format by which sounds and sound effects for synthesizers and computers can easily be loaded and exchanged between various instruments.

Of course, these things are a long and complicated stretch from what MIDI was originally conceived to do. For the beginning MIDI user, only a small portion of the MIDI specification is useful and important as you make music with MIDI at home.

What Is MIDI Today, And What Does It Mean To Me?

Today, MIDI is almost synonymous with personal computers. When we speak of MIDI, computers, software, sequencers, audio and other computer-related applications immediately come to mind. Interestingly, desktop computers were not an established concept when MIDI and the early electronic musical instruments were conceived.

Little did the creators of MIDI know that the personal computer revolution would allow people to use their desktop computers to interface with and eventually control many instruments at a time, creating a virtual multitrack recording studio in any home.

The personal computer revolution changed MIDI in many ways. It enhanced its design and specification, and brought it to the forefront of computer music. It allowed MIDI and MIDI instruments to do more than ever hoped.

Why Do I Need MIDI?

At this point you are probably saying, "Why do I need MIDI?" The simple answer is, "It depends on what you want to do, and what equipment you plan to use to achieve your musical goals."

In a way, MIDI and MIDI instruments are ecumenical — they can be used by hobbyists and professionals alike. Whether you use MIDI or not doesn't depend on your type or level of musical application. It has more to do with: 1) what you want to do; and 2) what instruments and equipment you will use to get there.

In general, whether you want to play back music on a computer using MIDI files from the Internet, or make sounds for your games, it is very likely that you will use MIDI. If you use an electronic musical instrument of any type to play, play back or record music, it is likely that you will use MIDI.

Don't worry about added cost with MIDI. If you have an electronic musical instrument and/or a computer, you are already almost there. At the most, you might spend another US $50-$100 to get started. You can spend more to get interfaced and running, but for 90% of the essential applications, no more financial investment is required.

If you are just starting to make music with your computer, MIDI may be built-in already. If not, this book will tell you how to find it, add it, and make music or play music in a snap.

If you have an electronic keyboard that has a built-in recorder (sequencer), or any electronic musical instrument and other MIDI devices, this book will explain how MIDI is used to make instruments and MIDI boxes work together without a computer. If you have a computer and a MIDI instrument, this book will also bring all the component parts together and explain how to play, compose, arrange and record music with MIDI.

Chapter Three

Types Of MIDI Instruments And Devices

With a little background and history under your belt, it's time to put your studio together, and make some music with MIDI. We will start with an exploration of MIDI to make sure we have the right equipment.

Even though different users and applications of MIDI have been mentioned, we all have to start in the same place. This chapter applies to everyone who will use MIDI, whether you will play yourself, or simply play back MIDI files that someone else has composed.

What Kind Of MIDI Devices Are There?

Let's to go back to the Virtual MIDI Museum. This time we are going to visit a different exhibit: "Electronic Musical Instruments and Computers that Make Music." By visiting this third exhibit we will: A) get a broad overview of the various types of MIDI gear; and, B) see ways in which MIDI gear can be used together.

This exhibit is cool and easy to check out. It is arranged by type of gear, and by year. It has a variety of working equipment that demonstrates the various generations of MIDI instruments. As you look through this exhibit, keep this in mind — every piece of MIDI equipment, no matter how simple or complex, has two distinct characteristics:

1. It produces sound electronically, or has a device that converts electric sound (like an electric guitar), or acoustic sound (like a piano), into digital or numerical (computer) information.

2. It has some kind of computer processing unit (CPU) inside. The CPU contains software that tells it what to do with that sound when linked to another MIDI device. It also allows it to be controlled by another MIDI device.

KEYBOARDS AND SYNTHESIZERS

The first type of instrument in the exhibit is the electronic keyboard. Its earliest generation, including MIDI, dates back to 1984. This includes the early synthesizers, big and small. As stated in the previous chapter, most of these instruments played only a single note at a time, others many.

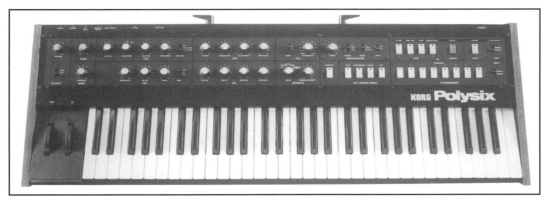

Figure 3.1 Korg Polysix

What were the distinguishing factors that set these instruments apart? How do you know these are MIDI instruments? Simple: they have the characteristic MIDI ports on the back (see Figure 3.2). These ports allow the keyboard to be connected to another keyboard, another MIDI device, or a computer. These instruments also have special software in them — functions and controls that can be set and configured depending on how the instrument is used. For instance, controls can be set to distinguish one instrument from any other MIDI instrument. These keyboards can be connected together, one can play another, and vice versa.

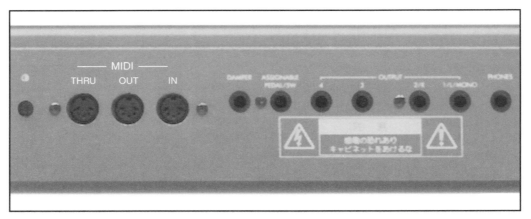

Figure 3.2 Back Of Keyboard With MIDI Ports

Some of the instruments in this exhibit are portable, others are not. In the early days of MIDI, keyboards designed to be used at home did not have MIDI. This was primarily due to cost and application. Keyboards for professional use almost always did support MIDI.

As MIDI evolved and became well-accepted, almost every type of electronic keyboard (a keyboard with lots of preset sounds that cannot be modified) and synthesizers (more complex electronic keyboard instruments that have a fully editable sound palette) all started to support MIDI. Other types of home keyboards, like auto accompaniment keyboards, also started to support MIDI. Most digital pianos, which make only a few sounds, but have excellent piano replications, also started to be designed with MIDI.

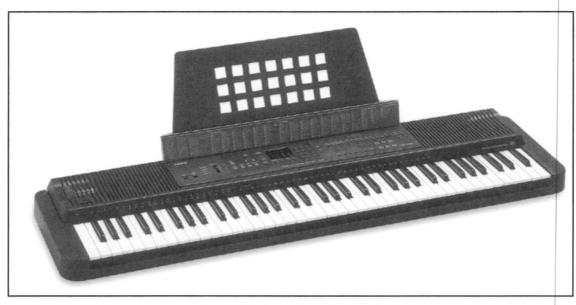

Figure 3.3 Casio Home Keyboard

Figure 3.4 Yamaha Auto Accompaniment Keyboard

In the late 1980s, new hybrid electronic keyboards called "music workstations" also appeared. They not only supported MIDI for performance, but contained MIDI recorders (called sequencers), drum machines, and effects processors within one instrument. These instruments used MIDI to allow communication with other MIDI instruments, and they also used parts of the MIDI language to allow on-board recording and playback of multitimbral (multi-part) performances.

Figure 3.5 Korg M1 Music Workstation

KEYBOARD CONTROLLERS

Time for another basic definition: controller. Up until now, every instrument mentioned was a keyboard instrument. Someone could sit or stand and play it. It had some kind of input device, namely keys, and when the keys were played, they sent signals to a CPU that made electronic sounds.

In the world of MIDI, there are lots of different types of controllers. A controller is an input device that takes a physical action, like pushing a key or plucking a string, and converts that performance to MIDI information. Often controllers, like synthesizers, have on-board sound generation. Occasionally, they don't. There are also some keyboards that are only controllers and make no sound. These will be explored later.

ALTERNATE CONTROLLERS

What other kinds of MIDI devices are there? They fall in two categories: A) alternate controllers; and B) other MIDI-compatible devices. Alternate controllers are non-keyboard instruments, like guitars or drums, that are electronic and have input devices. This means that you can play them and make music using MIDI to control other MIDI devices.

One popular example is the MIDI guitar. This is a guitar that has pickups and a computer that convert notes played into digital information. MIDI guitars have synthesizer modules connected to them that take the audio information sent from the guitar strings and create new synthesized electronic sounds. For the most part, the guitar and module don't use MIDI, but a specialized technology created just for that electronic guitar. The specialized synthesizer attached to the guitar, which makes the sound, is MIDI-capable, and itself can send and receive MIDI information.

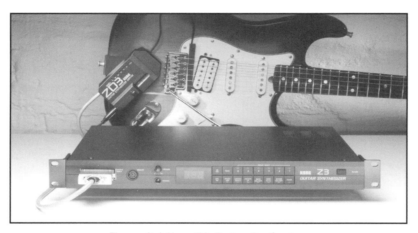

Figure 3.6 Korg Z3 Guitar Synthesizer

A hybrid of this technology has also become very popular. Guitarists with an acoustic or electric guitar can now attach a special pick-up (mic) to their instruments and make music with MIDI. The pick-up is attached to a little computer that converts notes to MIDI messages. That converter then interfaces with a synthesizer to make sound, and can also be connected to a computer. Some major guitar companies even ship their electric guitars with a special fitting that allows easy connection to MIDI devices for easy computer connection.

From there, the permutations of traditional acoustic instruments that support or can be converted to support MIDI are never-ending. There are drum controllers that send MIDI information, other percussion instruments with keyboards, a myriad of stringed instruments, electronic wind instruments, and more. Believe it or not, there are even vocal MIDI devices that can be connected to a standard vocal microphone.

Figure 3.7 Kat Drum Controllers

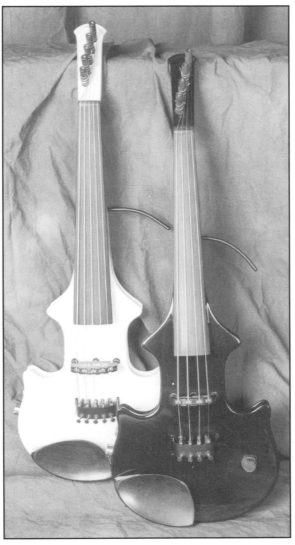

Figure 3.8 Zeta MIDI Violin

Figure 3.9 Korg ih Vocal Harmonizer

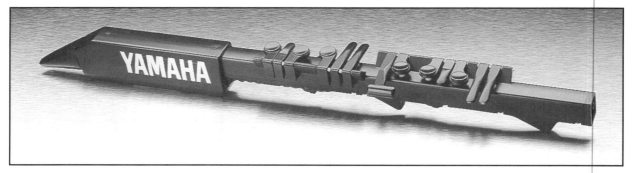

Figure 3.10 Yamaha WX7 Wind Controller

There have also been many unique MIDI performance devices, or controllers, that have come and gone. The more popular include the drum machine, a small box with small pads that play prerecorded percussion patterns and allow new drum patterns to be composed.

Figure 3.11 Roland Drum Machine

KEYS VERSUS ALTERNATE CONTROLLERS

At this point you may be asking why the electronic keyboard was the first type of instrument to widely support MIDI.

Why keyboards first, and all these other instruments second? The simplest explanation is design. First, MIDI was initially conceived and developed around synthesizers with keyboards. Second, the physical design of synthesizers, electronic keyboards and music workstations allows easy integration of the extra computer components required to support MIDI (like the interface ports, computer information, programming).

Moreover, electronic keyboards and synthesizers are electronic. The sound they create is made by a computer tone generator first. When a key is pressed, it sends a note number to a computer, sound is generated, and it plays. There is no conversion of an acoustic (analog) note, like a string plucked on a guitar or violin, to digital information.

Lastly, the electronic keyboard is more portable than alternative controllers. The "input devices" (the keys) are small and compact. All of the computer components that input the notes, make the sound, interpret the notes as MIDI information, and play the notes aloud, fit in one case.

With alternate controllers like wind instruments and guitars, the player sometimes stands, sometimes sits, and almost always needs to move with larger, more exaggerated movements to emulate performance on the acoustic counterpart. Most importantly, the way the sound is produced and converted to digital information is more complex than with an electronic keyboard.

OTHER TYPES OF MIDI DEVICES

Aside from keyboard and alternate controllers, what else is there? There are a host of strange and unusual instruments, and some widely used devices that we have yet to explore.

First, the more popular:

1. **MIDI Controller Keyboard:** This is a "dummy" keyboard — a MIDI keyboard that has no sound generator or synthesizer. Its only purpose is to translate played notes to MIDI information. This information is sent to another device, like a synthesizer module or computer.

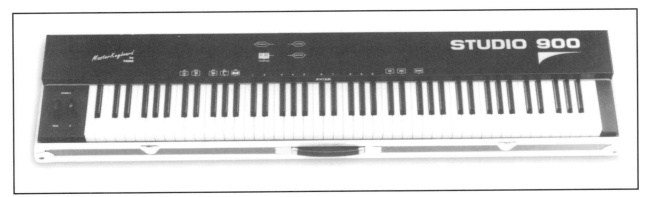

Figure 3.12 Fatar Controller

2. Synthesizer Modules: This category is important. It is a synthesizer with no keyboard, a box full of sounds. It is intended to be used with a MIDI controller keyboard as a primary sound generator, or as a secondary sound generator, to augment the sound palette of another MIDI keyboard, guitar controller, or computer.

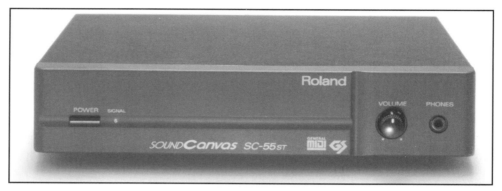

Figure 3.13 Roland Sound Canvas Module

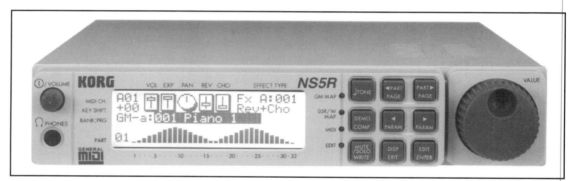

Figure 3.14 Korg NS5R Module

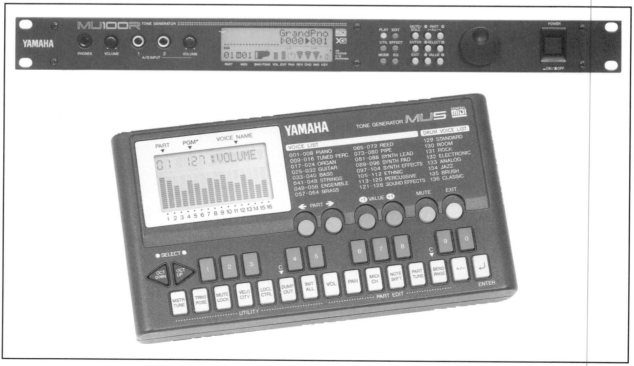

Figure 3.15 Yamaha MU100R and MU5 Modules

3. Effects Processors and other Enhancement Devices: These are MIDI-capable devices that are not synthesizers. The most popular are effects devices, boxes that enhance sound signals, like a box that adds reverb to a vocal part, or a guitar FX processor that adds distortion to an electric guitar line.

4. Stand-Alone Sequencers: These are also MIDI devices. Sequencers are digital multitrack recorders and are a very important application of MIDI.

There are other more unusual and outrageous boxes that were created to be MIDI devices, and there are other traditional musical devices that have been retrofitted to support MIDI. For instance, many standard audio mixers have MIDI support so that they can be automated for use with other MIDI instruments and computers. At the other end of the spectrum are many wild devices used in theater and stage performances, like MIDI-controllable lighting consoles and FX devices.

Figure 3.16 Mackie Mixer With MIDI Capabilities

Chapter Four

Getting Started

WHAT KIND OF MIDI DEVICE(S) DO I NEED?

What kind of devices do you have already? Electronic keyboard or synthesizer, guitar MIDI controller, electronic wind instrument, computer? You have to have at least one of these devices to make music in conjunction with MIDI. More likely, you will need two. Remember, MIDI is an interface for interconnecting music technology gear. Unless you have a music workstation or a computer with built-in hardware (like a sound card) or software synthesizer (like QuickTime or a plug-in synth for your Web browser) to make music using MIDI, you will be interconnecting two or more of the above.

The goals for this chapter are to:

- Identify the gear that you have now
- Determine if anything is missing
- Connect your home music gear properly
- Make some sound!

WHAT ARE THE BASIC COMPONENTS?

In order to get started, you need to know what a few basic types of equipment are. In addition to the MIDI performance instruments identified in the previous chapter, you will need to have:

I. MIDI Controller: This could be a synthesizer, electronic keyboard, guitar controller, or MIDI keyboard controller. Remember that if you have a keyboard controller that has no sound generator (no sounds built-in), then you also have to have a sound module or sound card in your PC.

II. MIDI Interface: If you are going to use a computer, you will need a MIDI interface to interconnect your controller to your computer. There are a few options:
    A. First check to determine whether your controller or any secondary module already has a built-in interface. Instrument manufacturers have recently started incorporating interfaces into their instruments. You may not need to buy one. If your instrument already has a MIDI interface, it will look like Figure 4.1.

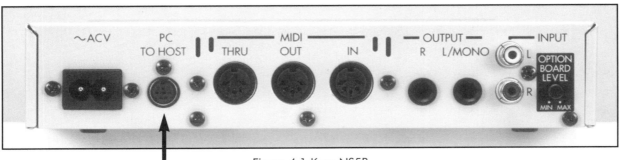

Figure 4.1 Korg NS5R

B. If your instrument doesn't have a built-in interface, then you will need one of the following:

1. For a PC: either a MIDI card to add to one of your open card slots, a sound card that supports MIDI via its game controller port, or an external interface.

Figure 4.2 Opcode MIDI Translator PC External Interface

2. For a Mac: an external MIDI interface.

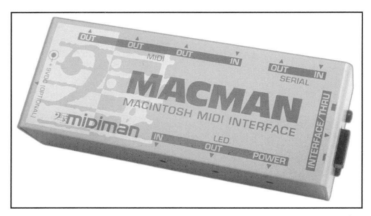

Figure 4.3 Macman MIDI Interface

C. MIDI cables: This is a basic requirement. Any time you interconnect MIDI instruments or peripherals, standard 5-pin DIN cables are used.

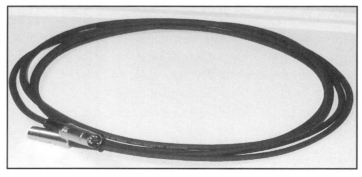

Figure 4.4 MIDI Cable

In addition, you may want to have, or may be able to use:

I. Secondary MIDI instruments: If you have a keyboard controller that has no built-in sounds, you will need secondary sound generators. In addition, you may add these devices to expand the number and variety of sounds that you have available. Secondary sound generators are often called "sound modules," and they come in many shapes and sizes. Here are a few examples:

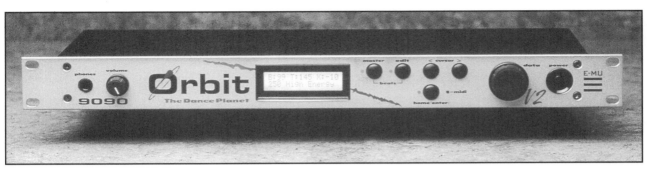

Figure 4.5 E-MU "Orbit the Dance Planet" Sound Module

Figure 4.6 Roland Sound Module

II. Computer: This is all that you need to start making music with MIDI, and it can be the device that you use to control all of your MIDI gear. It can be a Mac or PC, and the system software should meet the following specifications, at a minimum:
   A. For a PC: Windows95
   B. For a Macintosh: Macintosh OS 7.5 or greater

III. MIDI drivers, extensions and software: If you have a computer, you will also need MIDI drivers (PC), extensions (Macintosh), and music software to enable your computer to communicate properly with your MIDI instruments. The types and instructions for properly loading and configuring your computer will be addressed in Chapter Five.

Setting Up Your Studio

There are a few most-used, and most easily configured MIDI set-ups. In order to determine if you have what you need to get started, fill out the following checklist:

Configuration	Controller	Module	Interface	CPU	Cables	Drivers	Other Software
1	Y	N	Y	N	Y	N	N
2	Y	Y	Y	N	Y	N	N
3	Y	N	Y	Y	Y	Y	Y
4	Y	Y	Y	Y	Y	Y	Y
5	N	N	*	Y	Y	Y	Y
			* Sound card may double as interface				

Figure 4.7 MIDI Setup Checklist

Here are the five essential configuration options:

Configuration 1: Controller To Controller
Configuration 2: Controller With Modules As Slaves
Configuration 3: Synth/Controller To Computer
Configuration 4: Synth/Controller And Modules To Computer
Configuration 5: Computer Only Or Computer With Sound Card

CONFIGURATION 1: CONTROLLER TO CONTROLLER

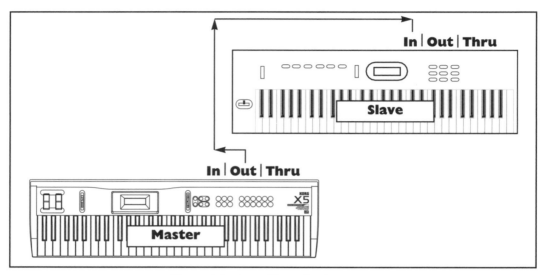

Figure 4.8 Master/Slave Configuration

This is the most basic configuration — the one for which MIDI was created in the first place. The simplest way to put it together is with two MIDI-capable instruments, like two electronic keyboards.

This is the appropriate time to introduce a very important concept in MIDI — master and slave. Whenever two or more pieces of MIDI equipment are interconnected, one must be designated as the "master," meaning "the boss." All other pieces of gear are subservient to the master. All notes are played at the master and all commands and instructions are sent from the master. All other equipment, the "slaves," are dumb partners. They receive notes and commands from the master, and are not able to send instructions, notes, or any other information to any other MIDI instruments.

With two MIDI keyboards in your studio, you have to decide which will be the master, and which the slave. The logical choice for a master is the instrument that has more capabilities.

To make the connection between your master and slave, you need only one MIDI cable. Since the master sends all the notes and commands, you need to connect a MIDI cable from the MIDI OUT port on the master to the MIDI IN port on the slave and . . . voila!

Once you have made the connections, test your work. To test, think about what has just been done. You have connected the OUT of your master to the IN of the slave, so what is happening? MIDI communication from MIDI instrument to MIDI instrument travels in one direction, like the audio signals to and from your home cassette player. MIDI data travel from your master (OUT) to your slave (IN). That's it. So if everything is connected well and turned on, play a note or two on the master. At the same time that you play and hear the notes from the master the slave plays them too!

It may be difficult to hear the difference, especially if the sounds selected on the master and the sounds selected on the slave are similar. To be absolutely certain MIDI data are traveling from the master to the slave, turn the volume down on the master (so you can't hear the master's notes) and turn up the volume on the slave. If all works correctly, the notes you hear will be heard from the slave, but played from the master.

What data travels from master to slave? Notes; notes ON (you press the key and it plays), and notes OFF (you release and the sound stops). If you have a pedal, a joystick or pitch and modulation wheels, that information travels from master to slave, too.

Figure 4.9 Switches And Volume Pedal

Of course, this configuration applies to other combinations of instruments. If you use an alternate controller, like a guitar, the same principles apply. If you want to use the guitar controller to send notes to a MIDI keyboard, you connect the MIDI OUT port on the guitar controller to the IN on the keyboard slave. Test your connections the same way. Turn down the volume on the guitar synth, turn up the volume on the keyboard slave, and what do you hear?

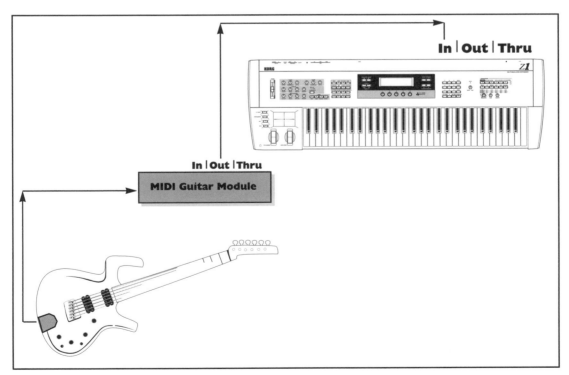

Figure 4.10 Guitar Controller To Keyboard Slave

CONFIGURATION 2: CONTROLLER WITH MODULE(S) AS SLAVES

This configuration is a variation on Configuration 1. The only difference is that instead of having two keyboards, or an alternate keyboard and a controller, you have one controller and a sound module (or several sound modules). The controller automatically becomes the master; the modules automatically become the slaves.

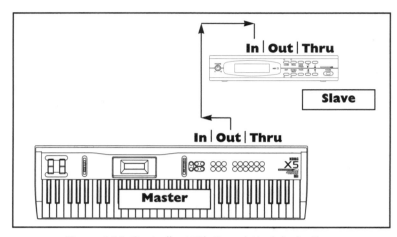

Figure 4.11 Controller With Sound Module As Slave

This configuration is the most sensible and economical, especially when compared to Configuration 1. Why? In Configuration 1, your slave was another controller instrument, but its controller functions weren't being used. For instance, with two controller keyboards, only the master sends notes or commands. The input device, or keys, on the second goes wasted.

Configuration 2, on the other hand, includes just one master controller, which is the instrument at which you play and send notes and other commands. The secondary module, the slave, receives notes and commands from the master and plays them.

Although we have only considered one master and one slave up until this point, there is practically no limit to the number of slaves that can be chained to a master. Suppose you have a master controller keyboard, and two or three modules, or slaves. You connect the master to slave 1 by connecting the MIDI OUT port on the master to the MIDI IN port on the slave. Then you chain slave 1 to slave 2 by connecting the THRU PORT on slave 1 to the IN PORT on slave 2. If you have a third device, do the same. Connect the THRU PORT on slave 2 to the IN PORT on slave 3.

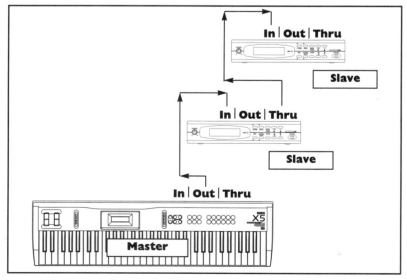

Figure 4.12 Multiple Slaves Chained To Master

"OUT to IN" makes easy sense in Configuration 1. MIDI information always flows from the master to its slave. When there is more than one slave, the concept is the same, there is just another device in the chain. The master always sends all data to all instruments. So if you play a note on the master, that one note is sent to slave 1, and a duplicate of that note goes to slave 2, too. The THRU port simply allows an exact copy of the data received at slave 1 to be passed to slave 2 as well. And, so on to slave 3, 4, etc.

If you have more than one slave, how do you test Configuration 2 to discover if it works? Adjust the volume on the master and slaves in succession, playing and turning each instruments volume up and down, one at a time. Do each of the slaves play notes as you perform from the master?

CHANNELS

Time for a brief diversion. It should be mentioned that turning volumes up and down is a crude way of testing whether your MIDI chain is properly connected. There is another way built into the MIDI specification, but it is a little more complicated to implement.

The provision built into MIDI that allows different instruments in a MIDI chain to be played independently is called "channels." Channels in MIDI are similar to channels on a television. Channels in MIDI allow different sounds to be played, while channels of a TV allow different programs to be played.

Of course playing MIDI instruments is a little different than playing programs on a television. Generally, you watch one channel on a TV at a time. Watching more than one, like the news, a sitcom and music television, at the same time, gets a bit confusing. With MIDI, more than one channel at a time is a good thing!

In MIDI only one instrument sound, or timbre, plays on one channel at a time. Music often requires many different instrument sounds to be played at a time, like a bass, a guitar, and a piano. To achieve more complex musical textures, many MIDI instrument sounds play on many channels at the same time.

How many different MIDI instrument sounds can be played at a time? It depends on how many MIDI channels there are. The MIDI specification provides for a maximum of 16 channels in a MIDI system.

BACK TO CONFIGURATION 2

So, in Configuration 2, if you wanted to play the master, slave 1, and slave 2 independently, each has to be set to a different channel. For example, we might use the following setup chart:

Instrument	Channel	GM Timbre
Controller	1	GM01 Piano
Slave 1	2	GM57 Trumpet
Slave 2	3	GM33 Wood Bass

Figure 4.13 Chart With Master On Receive Channel CH1/G,
Slave 1 On RCH2, And Slave 2 On RCH3

To start, the master should, by default, be set to channel 1. Set slave 1 to receive channel 2 messages, and slave 2 to receive channel 3 messages. If you don't know how to change MIDI receive channels, refer to the owners manuals for the controller and slave(s). Look in the glossary at the back of the manual. Anything to do with "channels" should lead you to the right place.

Next, you must turn LOCAL off on your controller (master). Why? LOCAL is a MIDI parameter that determines whether notes played at your controller are actually sent to the tone generator inside. If LOCAL is OFF, then your controller's built-in sound generator won't receive any note messages; consequently, it won't play sounds internally.

When LOCAL is off, don't worry about turning the volume ON or OFF, UP or DOWN on your controller, because no MIDI messages are being sent to its built-in sound generator. It won't make sounds internally.

Now we can concentrate on the slaves. Make sure that the volume level on each of the slaves is set to a comfortable listening level. If you don't know what a comfortable level is, you should set their volumes at "0" and slowly increase the volume to a comfortable level as you play from the master.

First test slave 1. Since slave 1 is set to receive notes on channel 2, you should set your controller to send channel 2 (see your owners manual). This may simply require setting the channel (send) to channel 2. Play. If all worked well, you will hear the trumpet sound playing on slave 1 as you play notes from your master.

Now test slave 2. It is set to receive notes on channel 3. Set your controller to send channel 3 and you should hear the bass sound play from slave 2.

If you want to hear your controller play (the piano sound), turn LOCAL ON, and set your send channel to 1. If you want all instruments, the controller and slaves, to play simultaneously, they must all be set to receive notes on the same channel.

CONFIGURATION 3: SYNTH/CONTROLLER TO COMPUTER

The most effective and common use of MIDI instruments is in conjunction with a computer. Although this was only part of the initial specification for MIDI, this application now prevails. In order to make this configuration work, you need a MIDI controller, computer and interface, and the appropriate cables.

Even though a vast majority of desktop computer systems in homes are PCs running a version of Microsoft Windows, there are a lot of Apple desktop systems used for music making. Music production and music education prefer this platform. Since both systems are used for MIDI, and the basic connection and set-up of a Mac and Windows system varies slightly, let's consider both.

WINDOWS PC SYSTEM CONFIGURATION

As long as your controller is MIDI-capable, and you have a PC, you are almost ready to make music with MIDI. As mentioned before, the only other essential requirements are:

- a MIDI interface or sound card that supports MIDI
- MIDI cables
- appropriate MIDI drivers for your hardware
- MIDI music software

The key peripheral component that will let you interface your MIDI controller with the PC is a MIDI interface. These vary in shape, size, quality, and price. For basic MIDI applications a simple interface with one or two INs, and three or more OUTs will do. The most common and inexpensive will provide a single IN and three OUTs. The INs and OUTs are called ports.

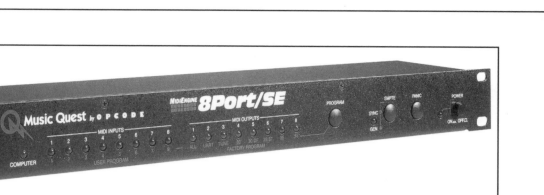

Figure 4.14 Opcode Musicquest Interface

As a PC owner, the number of ports are no less important than the physical type of interface that you select. Because Windows PCs are modular in design, you have a couple of options: an internal card that must be physically installed in your PC; or, an external MIDI interface that is connected to an open serial or parallel port on your computer. Furthermore, if your PC has a sound card, or you plan to purchase a sound card for games, most of these devices have MIDI interfaces as well.

Is one option better than another? Not really. It depends on your needs and the capabilities of the PC. For the goals and objectives of this book, any one will do.

Once you have identified the MIDI interface that you intend to use, it is time to make the connections. If the MIDI interface is internal (sound card or interface card) you connect the OUT port on the MIDI controller to the IN port on your card. Then connect the IN port on the MIDI controller to the OUT port on the card.

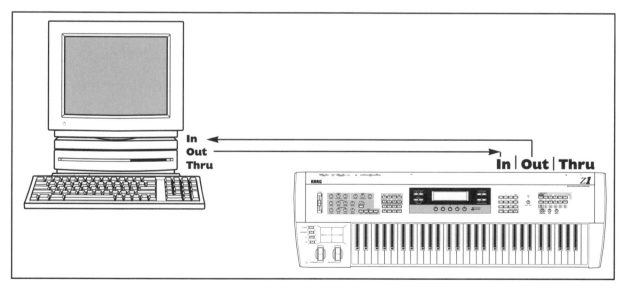

Figure 4.15 Standard PC Connections

There may be an exception or two to the above configuration. Many sound cards and some MIDI interfaces have an alternate port for MIDI connections. Instead of the standard IN and OUT ports, there exists a standard PC connector, like the DB9 port shown on the SoundBlaster card in Figure 4.16. In this case, you make one connection at the PC card, and plug the IN and OUT connectors into your MIDI controller.

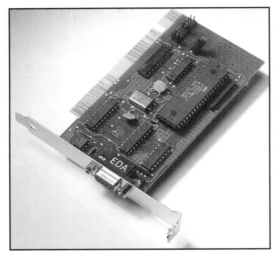

Figure 4.16 SoundBlaster Card

If you have a sound card that supports MIDI, are there situations when you would still use an independent MIDI interface card or external MIDI interface? If you connect a game controller, like a joystick or track ball to the sound card, then that port is no longer available for MIDI. If that is the case, you must change drivers and cables each time you switch from game playing to music making, an annoyance to say the least. For advanced MIDI applications, MIDI users often prefer more sophisticated interfaces dedicated to music making. These interfaces often sport more ports, access to more than 16 MIDI channels, and more flexible, independent control of multiple MIDI devices.

The last option for PC users is the external interface. If you have no card slots available, or you use a laptop that doesn't have slots, then you must resort to an external interface. This type plugs into an available serial or parallel port on your PC with the appropriate cable. You then plug the IN port on the card to the OUT port on the MIDI controller. Then connect the OUT port on the card to the IN port on the controller.

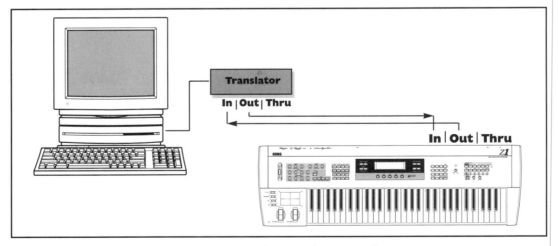

Figure 4.17 PC With External MIDI Interface

APPLE MACINTOSH SYSTEM CONFIGURATION

Apple Macintosh computers are a bit simpler to interface with MIDI-capable musical instruments. They are what computer users and manufacturers call true "plug and play." For the most part, all you have to do is plug an external MIDI interface, like Opcode's Translator II, into one of the Mac's serial ports (modem or printer). Then, like in the other configuration, connect the IN port on the interface to the OUT port on the MIDI controller, and the OUT port on the interface to the MIDI controller's IN port, and you are done.

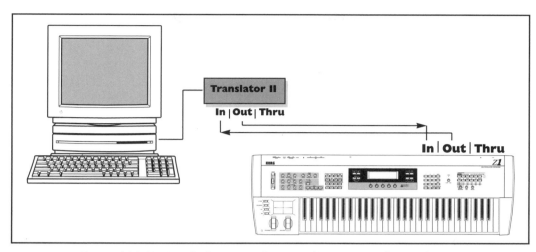

Figure 4.18 Macintosh Computer Connected To An Opcode Translator II

Both the Mac and PC configurations require basic software, called extensions or drivers, to optimize MIDI use with other software programs. Drivers, extensions, their types, installation options, and their use will be discussed in Chapter Five.

CONFIGURATION 4: SYNTH/CONTROLLER AND MODULES TO COMPUTER

This is a simple extension of the previous computer examples. If you have not read Configuration 2, "Controllers with Modules," do so now.

If you have properly connected your PC or Mac and MIDI controller via the computer interface, you are almost finished. Depending on the type of MIDI interface you have, you may choose one of the following options:

- If you have a MIDI interface with only one OUT port, take any additional devices, the slaves, and chain them to your master controller. As in Configuration 2, chain by taking a MIDI cable and connecting the THRU port on the MIDI controller to the IN port on slave 1. If you have another device, take a MIDI cable and connect the THRU port on slave 1 to the IN port on slave 2, and so on.

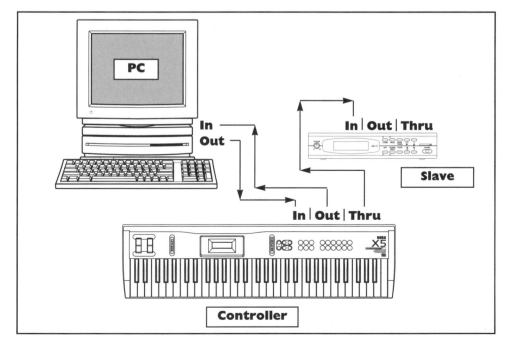

Figure 4.19 PC With Interface, Controller And Slave

• If you have a MIDI interface with multiple OUT ports, you can improve the performance of your setup by plugging your slaved devices directly into the interface, OUT from the interface to IN on the slave(s).

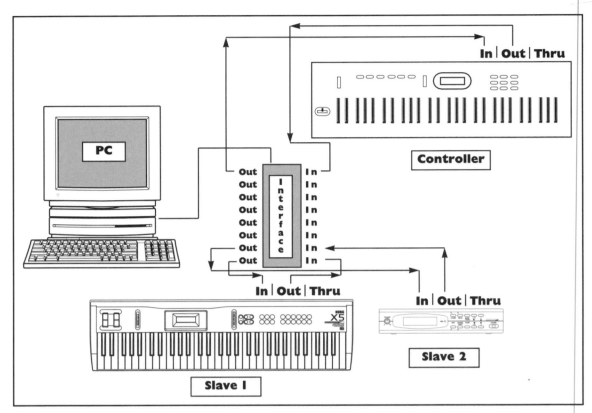

Figure 4.20 Interface With Multiple OUT Ports With Master And Slaves Connected

CONFIGURATION 5: COMPUTER ONLY, OR COMPUTER WITH SOUND CARD

Last but not least, you can make music with MIDI using only a computer. Some software is required. If your PC came with a sound card, or you later installed one, you already have a built-in synthesizer on the card. The card will contain a bank of General MIDI sounds.

If you have an Apple Macintosh computer with a current version of Apple's system software, QuickTime was added on installation. QuickTime Musical Instruments are a standard bank of sounds contained in a software-synthesizer that can be added to your system software. If you have a PC and no sound card, you can also use QuickTime for Windows. QuickTime is freely available on the Internet for download and installation from Apple Computer at: http://www.info.apple.com.

QuickTime for Windows is freely available for download also, and is a commonly accepted multi-media driver for video and audio. It won't let you use QuickTime Musical Instruments as a sound generator for MIDI, but it will play MIDI files embedded in Web pages.

Chapter Five 5

Computers And MIDI

Music making, technology and MIDI are practically synonymous. Today people delegate much of their music making and MIDI work to the computer. Their controller and sound devices are left mostly to making and performing sounds, and the computer does all of the busy work, like recording, playing back, editing, scoring, and arranging music.

This chapter focuses on the computer owner. If you have a computer, PC or Macintosh, and are hoping to make music using MIDI, this is where it all starts. We assume that you finished the "Getting Started" Chapter Four, and have properly connected all of your cables and hardware as described in pages 23-34.

In this chapter, you will:

- select the appropriate MIDI driver(s) or extensions for your computer platform and application(s)
- download any drivers or extensions required from the Internet (if you don't have access to the Internet, you will have to contact the manufacturer or a music dealer directly)
- install the drivers or extensions
- download one or two programs that can play MIDI files
- download a Standard MIDI File (SMF)
- test your system

Windows Or Macintosh — Does It Matter?

Before getting down to technical matters, let's preface this chapter by answering a popular and very common question. Does it matter what kind of computer I use to make music? The answer is, "No."

As we mentioned early on in this book, MIDI is a standard for interfacing music technology devices and computers. It runs equally well on a PC or Mac, and the platform you are using as you read this book doesn't matter.

If you have yet to commit to a computer platform for music making, the biggest determining factor in selecting a platform has nothing to do with your MIDI or computer hardware — it has to do with the musical goals that you plan to achieve. Thankfully, whether you want to play MIDI files, or record/sequence, score, or create multimedia projects, most of the major software manufacturers author their MIDI applications for both the Mac and Windows operating systems. If a manufacturer doesn't offer a cross-platform application, you can generally find a reasonable substitute from a competitor.

As important, consider with what platform you are already familiar. If you are a Macintosh user for business purposes, you may want to stick with the Mac for music. If you use a Windows PC in your office, use a Windows machine for music making. Unless you are a high-end user with very specific musical tasks to achieve, you might as well use a computer that you know well. When making music with MIDI, like any other technology-related application, you will have to do some technical troubleshooting from time to time. If you know Windows95 well because you use it at work, you will spend less time troubleshooting and more time making music in your studio.

Have You Installed Any Required MIDI Or Sound Card Drivers?

Before getting too deeply into specializing your computer's operating system for music making, there are a couple of issues that must be addressed. If you properly completed the setup of your computer in Chapter Four, you have a MIDI card, sound card or some kind of MIDI interface in your MIDI configuration. Depending on the type of hardware MIDI interface you have selected, you likely were given software with your interface or sound card when you purchased it.

FOR PC USERS RUNNING WINDOWS

If you are a PC user running Windows, carefully peruse the documentation that came with your MIDI interface or sound card. It has drivers, or small pieces of software that enable your computer to handle specialized tasks like using add-on gear (like a MIDI card). For your MIDI interface or sound card to work properly special drivers must be installed.

If you haven't installed any drivers, or don't know if you have, then locate the installation disks that came with your interface or sound card, locate the section in the device's manual on "Installation," and follow it carefully. In Windows95, most drivers are installed through the Control Panel. In the Control Panel you will find the "Add New Hardware Wizard." Start the Wizard, and it will ask you a variety of questions and step you through the process of installing any sound card or MIDI interface drivers needed. Be sure to read and follow the instructions for driver installation contained in the device's manual in order to avoid trouble.

Once the required drivers are installed, you must tell Windows95 what MIDI devices and driver you intend to use most of the time. In the Control Panel, select "Multimedia Properties," and then select the "MIDI" sub-menu. If the MIDI driver was installed properly, you will see it in the dialogue window. Select it, and then press the "Add New Instrument" button. If you have a sound card, select "External MIDI Port" if you have connected a MIDI instrument to it. Or, if you have no MIDI instrument, and want to use the synthesizer built into your sound card, select the driver for it.

In the next window, you have a choice. Select the driver for your MIDI card or instrument if you have one, or select "External MIDI Port" for your sound card. Select the button "Next," and then select "General MIDI Instrument." Lastly, select "Next" one more time, and then type the name of your General MIDI instrument. You are now finished.

FOR APPLE MACINTOSH USERS

If you are a Macintosh user, you probably don't need to install anything. The music software programs that we download later, or that you have already, talk to your interface without any special added drivers. If you have a professional multi-port interface, it may have come with special extensions; follow the detailed instructions for installation of software for your interface if this is the case.

Picking A MIDI Traffic Cop

If you are like 95% of the music and MIDI users, you will use many different MIDI programs on a regular basis. You will use one program to record, another to generate accompaniments with which to jam, another to print out scores of your work, and so on. As you build your MIDI system and select programs, it is best to pick music software that works well together. Otherwise, you may experience a few computer lock-ups. You may also change from one music software program to another without restarting your computer, losing MIDI communication with your instrument and losing sound.

To avoid this type of difficulty, there are a couple of different "MIDI traffic cops," or operating system extensions, that you can add to your computer, either Macintosh or Windows PC. These "traffic cops" are extensions to your computer's operating system that handle all MIDI communications in the background for you, and at the same time add some special functionality that makes MIDI work easier and friendlier — just like a traffic cop who directs traffic at a busy intersection. These extensions also have easy setup options that take care of configuring your computer and MIDI gear for you.

Most universally accepted is Opcode's OMS, or "Open Music System." Also commonly used is Mark of the Unicorn's "FreeMIDI." OMS is more frequently used on both PC and Mac since many Microsoft and Apple software developers have adopted it as a standard. On the PC, these "Traffic Cops" act more like standard drivers for their respective authors' software. On a Mac, they act like universal drivers that talk to one or many software programs and MIDI instruments at the same time.

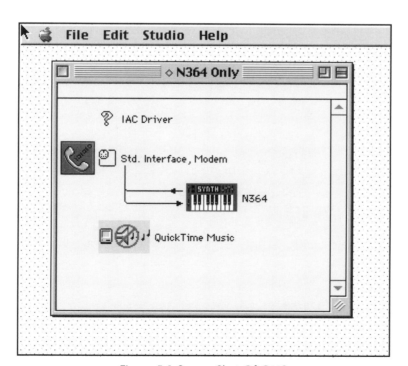

Figure 5.1 Screen Shot Of OMS

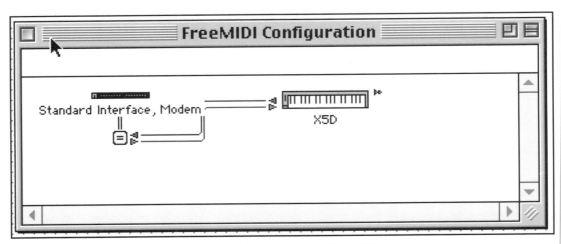

Figure 5.2 Screen Shot Of FreeMIDI

For Macintosh users, a third frequent often encountered option is Apple's MIDI Manager. This was Apple's first "MIDI Traffic Cop." It is not as friendly as OMS or FreeMIDI, and is not as reliable.

Which "MIDI Traffic Cop" should you select? The one that works with all or as many of the music applications you plan to use as possible. As a Macintosh user, if you plan to use a variety of MIDI music software from different manufacturers, OMS is probably the best bet. Why? Because of its wide acceptance, more music software developers for Macintosh support OMS than any other. Check MIDI compatibility for each of the software programs that you select or own before making your final choice.

FINDING A MIDI TRAFFIC COP

Most music software will come with OMS, MIDI manager, FreeMIDI or some other MIDI extension. This is the extension recommended by the manufacturer, but the program probably supports more than one extension.

For the sake of discussion in this book, we will go to the Internet and download Open Music System (OMS) to get started. Open your Web browser, like Netscape Navigator or Internet Explorer, and go to the following Web site: http://www.opcode.com/.

Once at Opcode's main page, go to their download area, look for OMS, and select the version appropriate for your computer. OMS is available at no charge, and you can download it directly from your browser via FTP. As you begin the download, be sure to give your browser a path and location in which to save the file where it is easily found. Put OMS in a folder with the rest of your music software.

SETTING UP OMS ON A MACINTOSH

The program will step you through the appropriate procedures for a successful configuration. Let's set up OMS now.

Double click or "open" on the OMS installer icon. The program launches, and you immediately see a dialogue box (a box on the screen with several options from which to choose). Although there are several custom options for installing, choose "New Easy Setup." This option is simplest. OMS Setup goes out to the available serial port(s) on your computer, sends a message to your MIDI interface, "shakes hands" with it, and discovers what kind of interface it is. OMS then shows you a new dialogue box.

If the dialogue box shows you a setup that includes your MIDI interface by name, or at least displays "standard interface," proceed. By pressing "Continue," OMS then goes out and sends a MIDI message through your interface, attempting to discover what MIDI controller or additional MIDI devices are connected in your configuration.

When finished, you should see a complete, "New Setup," which identifies all of the gear properly connected in your setup. To test your system, go to the "Studio" menu, pull it down and select "Test Studio." Move your cursor over any of the musical instruments in the studio. It will turn to a "note-head" and as you click on devices in your studio setup, and a cluster of notes will play loudly.

SETTING UP OMS ON A PC

If you are a PC owner running Opcode software, OMS is required. If you don't own or use Opcode software, OMS is likely not needed by non-Opcode music programs, because they will use the MIDI drivers installed for your MIDI interface or sound card.

If you are a Windows PC owner and choose to install OMS, the installation procedures are similar. If you installed Opcode software, OMS already resides on your PC. If you don't have OMS, or need to install the latest version, go to Opcode's Web site listed above and download it. Once on your hard drive, install/setup OMS, and then run the application. OMS automatically checks the existing Multimedia Properties in Windows95, and checks to see if the General MIDI instrument you named is available. You can test to determine if OMS is running properly by pulling down the "Studio" menu, and selecting "Test Studio." Your cursor turns to a "note head," and you can drag it over your GM instrument's icon in the studio screen and click. If all is configured properly, you will hear notes sound on all 16 channels of your MIDI instrument or sound card tone generator.

TROUBLESHOOTING

What could go wrong? A variety of things. If OMS cannot locate your MIDI interface, or one or more of your MIDI devices, then consider the following before you panic:

- You don't see a MIDI interface: Are you sure you have properly connected all cables? If you are using a Windows PC, are the drivers and Multimedia Properties set correctly?

- You don't see one or more of your devices in the Setup window: If the MIDI interface is there, but nothing else, the MIDI cables are probably connected to the wrong port(s) on one or more MIDI instruments in your studio.

- Devices appear but they don't match your MIDI instrument names (for example, you see a keyboard icon with the title, "Modem." This is not a big problem. OMS knows that there is a MIDI device, it simply doesn't know its name (maybe the instrument is newer than this version of OMS). Double click on any device with an improper title, and a dialogue box appears with various manufacturers' names, model numbers, and an option to type in a unique name if unrecognized.

Most importantly, for Apple Macintosh computer users, are there conflicting extensions in the current system extension set? Whether you are experiencing problems getting MIDI to talk with various devices through OMS now or not, it is a good time to check if multiple MIDI extensions coexist on your computer; if they do, all but one should be turned off. For Macintosh users, go to the Extensions Manager (Apple Menu * Control Panels * Extensions Manager) and open it. Look through the extensions list and see what drivers are currently active (if an extension has a check mark next to it, it is active). If you are using OMS, then the OMS extension and OMS Preferred device should be active, and things like FreeMIDI and MIDI manager should be turned off. If you are using MIDI Manager, OMS and FreeMIDI should be turned off.

OTHER BENEFITS OF OMS

As you can see, using a program like OMS takes some of the mystery out of MIDI — this is a good thing. It is a "smart" program which handles the basic configuration of your MIDI gear, ensuring that it works properly together. FreeMIDI does the same.

There are other benefits as well. OMS and FreeMIDI support a variety of different MIDI instruments, providing name support for the hundreds or thousands of names contained in any given instrument. For example, see Figure 5.3, which shows a typical MIDI sequencer called Master Tracks Pro by Passport Designs. Using OMS as the preferred MIDI driver, and because OMS recognizes the MIDI controller used in this studio, a list of all the sounds (patch names) in this instrument are available at a touch of a button. If OMS did not recognize this instrument, or you were not using OMS, you would be able to create a unique list of patch names for this instrument yourself, from scratch.

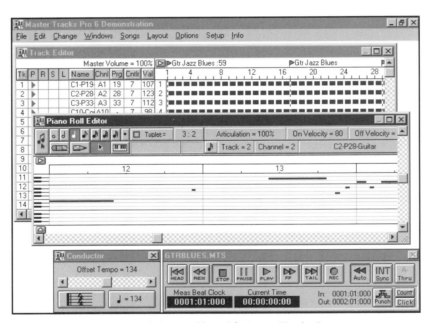

Figure 5.3 Screen Shot Of Master Tracks Pro

Lastly, your "MIDI Traffic Cop" monitors all MIDI communication in the background, so that you don't have to worry about it. And it does this for different music programs, as long as it is selected as the MIDI driver in the "setup" and/or "preference" options of all MIDI music programs that you are using.

Testing Your Studio Setup

There are a couple of ways to get started playing MIDI files. The easiest thing to do is download a MIDI file from the Internet, and play it from the Macintosh OS or Windows. Let's test the system in two ways, for both Macintosh and for Windows PC.

Before you do anything, you need a standard MIDI file (SMF) to play. Go to the Internet and visit an Internet site that contains publicly available MIDI files in standard MIDI file format. To find one, open your browser, visit your favorite search engine, like Yahoo, AOL Search or Excite, and search for "MIDI files."

http://www.yahoo.com/
http://www.excite.com/
http://www.search.com/

Pick a site, select any tune that you like, and download it. Put it somewhere on your hard drive where it can easily be located. Creating a folder entitled "MIDI Tunes" in your hard drive's "Music " folder is a good idea.

FOR WINDOWS PC USERS

Playing the MIDI file through your PC is easy once the appropriate drivers are loaded, and the "Multimedia Properties" are set in the Windows95 Control Panel. Go to the Start Menu on the Windows Task Bar, and select Programs • Accessories • Multimedia • Media Player. Open the Media Player, and select MIDI Instrument as your Device for playback. A dialogue window will open and prompt you for a MIDI file to play.

Locate the SMF that you downloaded from the Internet (inside the "Music" folder, inside "MIDI Tunes"), and open it. Press play on the Media Player's transport controls, and you will hear the tune!

FOR APPLE MACINTOSH USERS

With a Macintosh, everything you need to play MIDI files is built into the operating system. And now that you have added OMS to your system, it gets even easier. First, go to the QuickTime Settings Control Panel (Apple Menu • Control Panels • QuickTime Settings). Once opened, the control panel provides several options. Under "Music" options (not CD auto play), select QuickTime Musical Instruments. QuickTime Musical Instruments are the built-in General MIDI (GM) timbres in the Apple operating system.

Let's play the file in two ways: 1) using the built-in General MIDI synthesizer, QuickTime Musical Instruments; and, 2) using your MIDI instrument and OMS.

To play any MIDI file, any time, you can open it in Apple's SimpleText, the word processor and text editor provided by Apple with its system software. This is fun and easy, because SimpleText comes with QuickTime translation, enabling it to play movies, sound files, and MIDI files, as well as record audio files.

Find SimpleText on your hard drive. If you don't know where it is, go to the Finder, type "command F" and find "SimpleText." Once opened, go to the File Menu, select Open, and using the dialogue box, locate the MIDI file (SMF) that you downloaded from the Internet. Select it, and SimpleText will ask you where it can save the SMF (.MID) file as a movie. Why a movie? Audio tracks and MIDI files are standard layers in QuickTime, which plays movies, among other things. In the case of this file, there is no picture, so QuickTime opens it as a movie with no graphics or images, just MIDI data.

Once the file is opened as a movie, a control bar appears (see Figure 5.4). The control bar is part of a standard QuickTime window; it just appears that the image, animation or movie is missing. Use the transport controls (play, forward, back, stop, like on your home stereo CD audio player), and start the MIDI file. What do you hear? Start, stop, reset and forward through the "movie," or MIDI sequences several times until you are comfortable manipulating the sequence.

Figure 5.4 QuickTime Control Bar

How was the fidelity of the playback? Sounds a little "cheesy" you say? You are absolutely correct. And this is one of the reasons external MIDI sound modules, sound cards and MIDI instruments exist. Good quality sound from a synthesizer requires a lot of computer memory. The amount of memory on a PC or Mac dedicated to QuickTime musical instruments is limited, and the fidelity of the instrument set suffers. Playback quality also depends upon the type of speakers on your computer. If you play back MIDI files from QuickTime musical instruments, through your portable computer or desktop computer speakers, it will sound poor. If you plug the audio output from your computer into a good pair of stereo multimedia monitor speakers, or a good headset, the improvement in fidelity will be marked.

Now let's make the SMF playback sound even better. Go back to the QuickTime Settings control panel once again, and this time select OMS as your instrument playback option. Return to SimpleText and play the "movie" again. The playback of the SMF now goes directly through your MIDI interface to your MIDI controller and/or sound module. Notice any difference with the playback quality?

Note: Be sure that as you play the file through OMS and your studio setup, it sounds similar to the arrangement poorly played through QuickTime Musical Instruments. The integrity of the tracks and arrangement should be similar, even though it should sound much better on your MIDI instruments. In order for the file to sound properly, your MIDI instrument assigned to the job of playing the file must be set to a "multitimbral playback mode." There are many different modes and names for this function depending on the instrument being used, so refer to your instrument's user guide or reference manual and determine how to set it to play General MIDI (GM) timbres. The bottom line is this: the MIDI instrument must be in some sort of multitimbral playback mode, not a performance mode. You need to hear all of the MIDI timbres by having all the playback channels available to you at once.

Congratulations! You have officially tested your MIDI system and successfully played back a MIDI file.

Chapter Six

Playing MIDI Files

In the previous chapter, we confirmed that your configuration worked properly. By downloading a simple MIDI file, we successfully played it using QuickTime musical instruments or your PC's sound card. We also played the file using your MIDI interface and your MIDI instruments.

Now let's explore in-depth the nature of your MIDI instrument, MIDI files, and General MIDI. At the same time, we will put your MIDI instrument or sound card to the test, exploring its sound palette, and its recording and playback capabilities.

In this chapter you will:

- download a demo version of a popular sequencer and/or MIDI file player
- further explore SMFs and your MIDI instrument
- manipulate instrument sounds and other elements of a sequence
- rearrange a MIDI file
- learn more about General MIDI
- save and export a MIDI file to share with someone else

Find A MIDI File Player

On the Internet, download a shareware MIDI file player or sequencer demo program. If you don't have Internet access, visit a friend who does. If you go to your favorite search engine and type in "MIDI file player," you will find several — some good and some not so good. You can also try downloading a demonstration version of a commercial sequencing program. If you have a commercial sequencer and have yet to use it or explore it well, you should use it for this exploration.

Most demos either allow you to work without saving the sequences you have done, or work for only a certain number of days or weeks before the program expires. For a list of prospective demo sites, see the resource list at the end of this book.

Once you have installed the MIDI file player or demo, you need to do some setup. Look for a "setup" option or a "preferences" option in one of the main menus of the program. There you will have to tell the program things like:

- what driver or extension you are using for MIDI
- what port you are using/where your interface is located (COM2, MODEM port, etc.)

Downloading SMFs

To download a MIDI file, you must go to a Web site that offers Standard MIDI Files (SMFs). SMFs are an extension of the MIDI specification, and provide a common MIDI sequence (song/recording) file format for both Windows and Macintosh computer users. A file format is simply a way of storing computer information that is recognized by one or more types of computers and/or software programs.

For the sake of discussion, let's download an SMF from one of the music software developer's sites or from one of the SMF archives on the Internet. For instance, Passport Designs publishes a site where its software users can post and share their sequences and scores with other users and the public (start at http://www.passportdesigns.com/ and look for the "@passport" page). Alternatively, you may search any of the many public domain MIDI file archives. Try one of the classical or jazz archives, for fun.

Select a tune for download. Your browser will ask you where you would like to store it. Once again, the best place is on your hard drive, inside your "MIDI Tunes" folder, inside your "Music" folder. After the download is complete, look inside the destination folder and see if it is there. The file should show up as an SMF, and should be named as the title of the tune. Note that on a Windows PC, you will likely see the name of the file with a ".MID" suffix (especially if you are looking at the folder in "list view"). Macintosh users may or may not see the .MID suffix, and it doesn't matter.

Let's play the new SMF on your hard disk and test your studio's MIDI playback capabilities. Go to your MIDI file player, and pull down the File Menu. Select "Open," and find the SMF on your hard drive. Open the file, wait a couple of seconds for the file to load, and then play it by pressing "PLAY" with your cursor.

You don't see the word "PLAY" on any button or menu in the program? That is very possible. You should look for a common sequencer or file player tool called the "transport controls." They look like the play, rewind, fast forward and stop controls that you find on your home cassette or CD player.

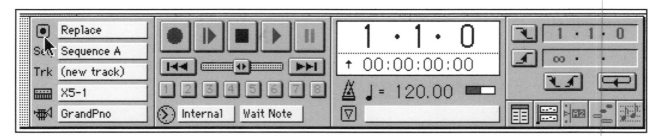

Figure 6.1 Sequencer Transport Controls Screen Shot

Carefully examine the various windows open in your MIDI file player. Locate the tracks window. Tracks are musical parts (performance information), occupying a specific MIDI channel. In the SMF that you are playing, how many tracks contain MIDI information? What sound is playing on each part? Are there drums playing in your sequence? On what track and/or channel do they reside?

More About SMFs

Now that you know how to find, download and play MIDI files, consider this: The files that you have loaded, Standard MIDI Files (SMFs), are actually a part of MIDI. A standard MIDI file is a file format — a standard way to save musical information. It is an extension of the MIDI specification created to allow musicians, arrangers and other MIDI users to exchange recorded MIDI music, sequence files, reliably.

Like other things that we have discussed regarding MIDI, an SMF is usable by all MIDI gear, and does not care what kind of computer it encounters. It can be opened generically by a Windows PC, a Macintosh, a music software program on either of these platforms, or any music workstation, stand-alone sequencer, or other device that is MIDI-compatible.

In short, a Standard MIDI File is a record of a MIDI performance. Any song, accompaniment or other composition created on a MIDI recorder, like a software program, can generally be saved as an SMF. A MIDI recording, or sequence, includes tracks of notes (performance), information about the sounds played, and other musical performance information, like speed (tempo), loudness (dynamics) and more. An SMF is a computer file that includes all of that same musical information in a simple, easy to read (by a computer or MIDI device) format.

There are a few variations of SMFs: Type 0, Type 1 and Type 2. Type 0 provides all the various parts and sounds in the MIDI sequence in one "fat," multitimbral track. Type 1 and 2 are multi-track, with the various parts retaining their track integrity when saved as an SMF. The types of SMFs are not essential for playing, saving and creating MIDI songs in this book. They may be important as you reapply the things you have learned as you become an experienced MIDI user and author.

WHERE TO FIND SMFs

There are many different places to find SMFs. As you are aware, you can download SMFs from the Internet. You can also purchase SMFs on disk from almost every major music publisher.

SMFs accompany most music methods today. For example, if you want to learn to play keyboard, keyboard method books sometimes are accompanied by SMFs. The files are examples of ideas and tunes presented in print in the music books, and often include accompaniments to which you can play and practice.

Many companies also sell SMF arrangements of popular songs to which people can play, perform and sing. These are called "music minus one" files, because one or more parts are missing or muted. You provide the missing parts by singing or playing.

Lastly, some companies provide MIDI clips, like "clip art" for graphic artists. MIDI clips can be used to add sound and interest to presentations and other multimedia productions and applications.

General MIDI

Back to your file. It is time to dig a little deeper into MIDI and your SMF in order to discover what can be manipulated, changed and modified.

One of the most basic elements of any MIDI file (SMF) is the palette of timbres, or instrument sounds, that are used. This is another standard component of the MIDI specification, called General MIDI.

When you first played the MIDI file you downloaded, you were asked what timbres, or sounds, made up the arrangement. Are there pianos, horns, strings, drums, new and unusual synthesized sounds that you have never heard before? Whatever sounds you find contained in an SMF, they all come from a part of the MIDI specification called General MIDI. General MIDI is a standard set of sounds devised by the MIDI Manufacturers Association (MMA). It is an important part of the standard that some consider a major benefit and others despise.

If you carefully investigated the sounds in your sound card, or the set of QuickTime musical instruments on your Macintosh, then you have a good understanding of what GM provides. General MIDI is a standard set of 128 sounds, plus drum kits. This set of sounds is divided into groups of eight, or octets, by family/type of sound (see Figure 6.2 for a complete list of the various instrument groups contained in GM).

GM Program List

1 : GrandPno	33 : WoodBass	65 : SprnoSax	97 : Rain
2 : BritePno	34 : FngrBass	66 : Alto Sax	98 : SoundTrk
3 : El.Grand	35 : PickBass	67 : TenorSax	99 : Crystal
4 : HnkyTonk	36 : Fretless	68 : Bari Sax	100 : Atmosphr
5 : ElPiano1	37 : SlapBas1	69 : Oboe	101 : Bright
6 : ElPiano2	38 : SlapBas2	70 : EnglHorn	102 : Goblin
7 : Harpsich	39 : SynBass1	71 : Bassoon	103 : Echoes
8 : Clavinet	40 : SynBass2	72 : Clarinet	104 : SciFi
9 : Celesta	41 : Violin	73 : Piccolo	105 : Sitar
10 : Glocken	42 : Viola	74 : Flute	106 : Banjo
11 : MusicBox	43 : Cello	75 : Recorder	107 : Shamisen
12 : Vibes	44 : Contra	76 : PanFlute	108 : Koto
13 : Marimba	45 : TremStrg	77 : Bottle	109 : Kalimba
14 : Xylophon	46 : Pizzicto	78 : Shakuchi	110 : Bagpipe
15 : TubulBel	47 : Harp	79 : Whistle	111 : Fiddle
16 : Dulcimer	48 : Timpani	80 : Ocarina	112 : Shanai
17 : DrawOrgn	49 : Ensmble1	81 : SquareLd	113 : TnklBell
18 : PercOrgn	50 : Ensmble2	82 : Saw Ld	114 : Agogo
19 : RockOrgn	51 : SynStrg1	83 : CaliopLd	115 : Stl Drum
20 : ChrcOrgn	52 : SynStrg2	84 : Chiff Ld	116 : WoodBlok
21 : ReedOrgn	53 : AahChoir	85 : CharanLd	117 : TaikoDrm
22 : Acordion	54 : OohChoir	86 : VoiceLd	118 : MelodTom
23 : Harmnica	55 : SynChoir	87 : Fifth Ld	119 : SynthTom
24 : TangoAcd	56 : Orch Hit	88 : Bass & Ld	120 : RevCymbl
25 : NylonGtr	57 : Trumpet	89 : NewAgePd	121 : FretNoiz
26 : SteelGtr	58 : Trombone	90 : Warm Pd	122 : BrthNoiz
27 : Jazz Gtr	59 : Tuba	91 : PolySyPd	123 : Seashore
28 : CleanGtr	60 : MuteTrum	92 : Choir Pd	124 : Tweet
29 : Mute Gtr	61 : FrenchHr	93 : Bowed Pd	125 : Telephone
30 : Ovrdrive	62 : BrasSect	94 : Metal Pd	126 : Helicptr
31 : Distortd	63 : SynBras1	95 : Halo Pd	127 : Applause
31 : Harmnics	64 : SynBras2	96 : Sweep Pd	128 : Gunshot

Figure 6.2 General MIDI Sound List

In addition, GM includes a definition for a drum kit, called a map. The drum kits (starting at GM129), are all mapped, or laid out, the same way. Each drum kit includes 52 drum sounds, and each sound is assigned a specific location, or key, on which it is to be heard.

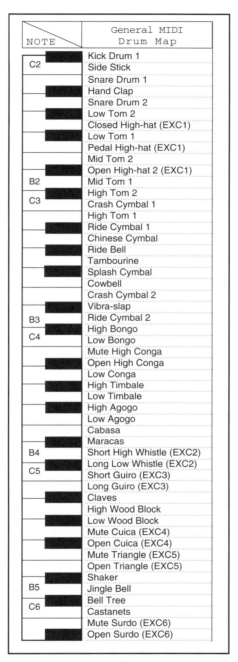

NOTE	General MIDI Drum Map
C2	Kick Drum 1
	Side Stick
	Snare Drum 1
	Hand Clap
	Snare Drum 2
	Low Tom 2
	Closed High-hat (EXC1)
	Low Tom 1
	Pedal High-hat (EXC1)
	Mid Tom 2
	Open High-hat 2 (EXC1)
B2	Mid Tom 1
C3	High Tom 2
	Crash Cymbal 1
	High Tom 1
	Ride Cymbal 1
	Chinese Cymbal
	Ride Bell
	Tambourine
	Splash Cymbal
	Cowbell
	Crash Cymbal 2
	Vibra-slap
B3	Ride Cymbal 2
C4	High Bongo
	Low Bongo
	Mute High Conga
	Open High Conga
	Low Conga
	High Timbale
	Low Timbale
	High Agogo
	Low Agogo
	Cabasa
	Maracas
B4	Short High Whistle (EXC2)
C5	Long Low Whistle (EXC2)
	Short Guiro (EXC3)
	Long Guiro (EXC3)
	Claves
	High Wood Block
	Low Wood Block
	Mute Cuica (EXC4)
	Open Cuica (EXC4)
	Mute Triangle (EXC5)
	Open Triangle (EXC5)
	Shaker
B5	Jingle Bell
C6	Bell Tree
	Castanets
	Mute Surdo (EXC6)
	Open Surdo (EXC6)

Figure 6.3 General MIDI Drum Map

Why is General MIDI so important? It provides a standard set of synthesized sounds with which composers, arrangers, computer game makers and multimedia producers can write music. Couldn't these folks always write with synthesizers and share their work? Yes, but they could not be assured that anyone playing their composition would hear what they wrote as they arranged it.

Keyboards, sound cards, synthesizers and other MIDI instruments are voiced for distinction. Every keyboard manufacturer is trying to outdo the other with the newest, latest, greatest and most unique sound. This keeps electronic music fresh and interesting. At the same time it sells instruments.

The problem with all of this differentiation between sounds comes when composers and arrangers try to share their work. For instance, I have the latest instrument from Korg, and have just written an exciting new song file in my NY studio. I hop on the Internet and e-mail the song file (SMF) to my partner in LA, who has the latest Roland instrument. She opens the file and plays it. Her reaction? What was he thinking when he wrote that file?!?

You see, the sounds in my instrument are completely different from the sounds in hers. Without a standard set of sounds, or both of us having the exact same MIDI instrument, we are out of luck. That is where GM comes in handy.

Many MIDI instruments, controllers, workstations and modules, and sound cards, now include, among their many sounds, the GM set of sounds. Look on the front panel of your MIDI instrument(s). If you see the GM logo, then that instrument is "General MIDI" compatible.

Figure 6.4 GM Logo

What does this do for you? If you are writing or arranging MIDI sequences or files using GM timbres, you can send them to any other person who has a GM instrument, and rest assured what they hear will be similar to what you composed or arranged. It helps publishers and authors create music and accompaniments for books that can be shared with many people (and eliminates the need to rearrange every song that you write for a thousand different MIDI devices). It also helps people who make multimedia presentations, games, and more.

GENERAL MIDI AND ITS VARIOUS PERMUTATIONS

As you download, play and share MIDI files, other file formats and banks of sounds (variations on GM) may come up, from time to time. Sometimes these formats and sounds are variations on the MIDI specification, and other times they are completely unique and have nothing to do with MIDI.

Instrument manufacturers and software developers have their own ideas on how to create and save sounds and sequencers that make their MIDI music tools special. Sound sets in MIDI instruments sometimes exhibit variation in type and arrangement. General MIDI is the accepted universal set of sounds. GM defines the variety of sounds and families of sounds to be shared, and the voicing of these sounds is well-defined. Regretfully, because the GM specification is so stringent, arrangers, composers and instrument makers also find it limiting.

Because of the limitations in General MIDI, a couple of manufacturers have created their own variation on the GM specification. For example, one of the most widely known is Roland's "GS" sound set. This format is commonly used by people who compose and play Roland instruments exclusively, and the additions and changes to GM are intriguing. On the other hand, this sound set is not widely supported by other manufacturers. In addition, there are many Internet browser plug-ins, software synthesizers that run in your browser, that are loosely based on GM. These are useful for playing sequences and sounds associated with a Web page, but may not conform to GM well.

EXPERIMENT WITH GM SOUNDS

With a better understanding of the GM bank of sounds, take a few minutes to play through many of them using your controller. You can do this by selecting an open track in a sequence and changing sounds from your MIDI file player or sequencer. You can also do this by working at your MIDI controller, in performance mode. Find the GM sounds, and start selecting them, by family, getting to know the characteristics of the various timbres.

Here are a few suggestions you may try as you experiment with the GM sounds:

- Play them loudly and softly.
- Play them in the low, middle and high ranges of the keyboard.
- As you play notes and sustain (hold them), try using the pitch and modulation wheels, or the joystick (your controller or GM keyboard is likely to have one or the other). Push and pull the wheels, or move the joystick in all directions in order to determine exactly how these controls affect various sounds.
- Use any pedals (like damper or expression) that you have to determine how they affect sounds, too.

Once you have gotten to know the GM sound bank pretty well, go back to your MIDI file player and start rearranging the file (SMF) that you played earlier. Try changing the timbres in various tracks. For example, if the sequence has a piano sound, change it to guitar. If the sequence has a horn sound, try changing it to a string sound.

MANIPULATE THE GM SOUNDS IN THE SMF

Using the MIDI file player or sequencer demo that you downloaded, dig-in to the SMF, and attempt to discover how many tracks exist in the file. What sounds are assigned to each track? If you don't see it, in one of the main menus of the player, there should be an option to explode track assignments. Open it. For example, see Figure 6.5, a window from Arnold's MIDI Player. In it you can see the GM location number and the title of each sound contained at the beginning of a sequence.

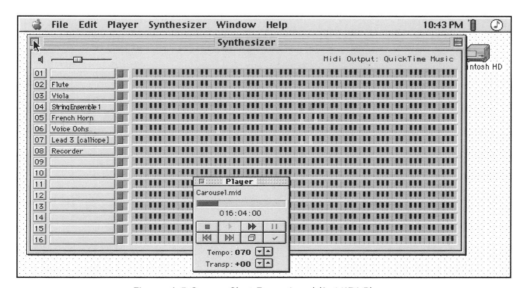

Figure 6.5 Screen Shot From Arnold's MIDI Player

Before you start to manipulate the sequence, take a few notes so that you can restore various settings in the SMF without starting from scratch. Record your findings in the following chart:

Part Name	Track	Timbre	Location	Channel	Notes

Figure 6.6 Track Setup Chart

Now, manipulate the tracks. Open the track assignment, and change the timbre. Have some fun. First, change the timbre assignments to sounds loosely related to the intended instrument sound. Then go wild, and select any outrageous sound you can imagine.

What other elements of MIDI can you manipulate? Here are a few suggestions, all of which are musical elements that translate into part of the MIDI specification:

- **Tempo:** Find the tempo, the speed at which the sequence plays back. This number is usually translated into beats per minute. For example, quarter note =120 translates into two beats, or ticks, per second. Slow down and speed up the tune by changing this setting.
- **Volume:** This is the general loudness of a track or particular instrument. In many sequencers and MIDI file players, this is manipulated like a mixing console.
- **Panning:** This is another component of the musical arrangement. It has to do with where sounds are placed in the stereo field (left ear to right ear in your headset).
- **FX:** Last element for now. FX = effects, or the ambient wash in which a synthesized sound is bathed. Sometimes this means reverb, other times chorus. There are a couple of effects settings contained within the General MIDI format.

The variety of musical elements that can be manipulated within an SMF player is fairly wide, but not quite as extensive as that which can be manipulated in a full-fledged sequencer. It is a good place to begin, though, and will provide a basic familiarity with MIDI that can give you the background necessary to jump into higher level sequencer software programs.

Continue to practice your SMF chops. Go back to the Internet, open a variety of files, and experiment with them. Keep an archive, or library, as you go along, saving interesting files that you can use in the future. By opening a variety of different sequence files, you are sure to gather lots of ideas about creating some of your own tunes, as well.

Let's Wrap It Up!

With any luck and a little bit of attention, you have become an expert MIDI user. As hinted in the beginning of this book, MIDI is not a complicated technology to master. It is a tool — a technology tool — for making music and music makers. The point of MIDI is to make music easier to compose, arrange and play back, with the help of electronic musical instruments and computers.

If you have breezed through this book, then it has served as a stepping stone to high-level music technology applications. It is time for you to pursue your passion; be it writing more music, scoring and arranging, or creating or playing music in multimedia technologies. Where should you go next? The Ultimate Beginner Tech Start Series™, from which this book comes, is filled with other great guides on how to make music at home — with computers, multitrack tape recorders, a sound system, and more. See the advertisement for other Ultimate Beginner Tech Start Series™ titles on the back cover of this book.

There is also an excellent reference list at the end of this book. It includes addresses and Web sites where you can learn about MIDI and music. The Internet is a fabulous repository of music and information on MIDI; from SMFs, to music technology information, to electronic musicians. You can even find discussion groups made up of people, like yourself, who make music with MIDI.

Enjoy MIDI and music. MIDI is a tool used to compose, create and enjoy music. If the world needs anything, it can always use a little more music, and technology makes that happen a little more quickly.

Glossary

Alternate Controller: Any MIDI device used as a controller that is not a standard keyboard or synthesizer.

Auto-accompaniment Keyboard: An electronic home keyboard that has built-in sounds and accompaniment patterns with which a user can play and improvise.

Channel: Any of sixteen data streams in MIDI where timbre, notes and other MIDI data reside in performance or playback.

Continuous Controller Data: A component of MIDI, like volume, pitch bend, or aftertouch, which can be manipulated almost constantly in performance, in very fine detail.

Controller: Any primary electronic musical instrument capable of sending a variety of MIDI performance information to a computer and/or other subsidiary MIDI devices.

Driver: A small piece of software that allows peripheral computer devices, like a MIDI interface, printer, or modem, to work properly with a personal computer; this term is more commonly associated with PC-compatible computers.

Effects Processor: An electronic music device that enhances or embellishes electronic or acoustic instrument sounds, by adding things like reverb, EQ, chorus, etc.

Electronic Keyboard: An electronic musical instrument which uses a piano-type keyboard as its primary performance input.

Extension: A small piece of software that enhances a computer's operating system. Most commonly associated with Apple Macintosh computers, extensions enhance software operation, or act as intermediaries between the computer and peripheral devices as well.

General MIDI: An extension to the MIDI specification the provides the basis for a standard set of 128 instrument sounds and drum kits.

Interface: In electronic music, a software and hardware specification that allows instruments and computers to work together.

Machine Control: An extension of the MIDI specification designed to allow electronic musical instruments and audio hardware to be synchronized.

Master: When referring to MIDI, the main controlling device to which all other devices in a studio or setup are subsidiary.

Metronome: In music and MIDI, the clock that keeps time, and all musical parts and tracks synchronized together.

MIDI Clips: Like clip art, MIDI clips are little MIDI tunes, mini sequences, that people add to multimedia presentations and Web pages.

MIDI Manufacturers Association: The music industry association that governs and publishes the MIDI specification.

Monophonic: A musical quality or constraint where an instrument can play only one note at any given time.

Monotimbral: A musical quality or constraint where an instrument plays, or a performance consists of, but one instrument sound.

Multitimbral: A musical quality or capability where an instrument plays, or performance consists of, more than one timbre at a time.

Musical Instrument Digital Interface (MIDI): A hardware and software specification created and commonly used in the music industry which allows various music technology devices, instruments, audio hardware and show equipment to work together.

Open MIDI System (OMS): A cross-platform driver or extension set for personal computers, Apple and Windows PC alike, that helps music technology equipment, software and computer hardware work together.

Panning: A MIDI control parameter pertaining to the location of an instrument sound in the stereo field.

Pedal: A MIDI control device, like a damper pedal or volume pedal.

Pitch Bend: A MIDI control parameter pertaining to very specific, and fine changes in pitch of a note played, and sustained.

Port: An input or output connection point between hardware devices.

Public Domain: Musical material, like songs, that have existed in general use for more than a specific number of years, and by law no longer require the payment of usage payments, or royalties, to the author or owner.

QuickTime: An Apple Computer software extension for Macintosh and Windows PCs that enhances multimedia playback of audio and video.

Sound Card: A peripheral or add-on device for PCs that includes a built-in synthesizer, or tone generator, and other multimedia functionality, like game controller support.

Sequencer: In electronic music, a computer software program, or stand-alone MIDI device that acts as a multitrack musical recorder and editor.

Show Control: An extension to the MIDI specification that allows MIDI devices to control, be controlled and interact with stage and lighting equipment for purposes of synchronized interaction.

Slave: When referring to MIDI instruments, a device that is controlled by another, namely a studio's or setup's MIDI controller, or Master.

Sound Module: An electronic musical instrument that contains a synthesizer, or tone generator, but must be controlled by another MIDI device (like a keyboard, or other alternate controller).

Standard MIDI File (SMF): An extension to the MIDI specification that provides a standard for saving and exchanging multitrack MIDI sequences, or performances in data form.

Synthesizer: An electronic keyboard, performance instrument, that allows the user to manipulate, edit and create his or her own unique sounds.

MIDI Time Code: An integral component in the MIDI specification that provides synchronization of musical performance events, as well as a basis for interaction with other standard time code generators for TV, video and audio.

Track: In MIDI, a musical part within a sequence.

Velocity: In MIDI, the speed at which a note is struck and/or released; often associated with volume.

Volume: A continuous control parameter that provides constant control and fine manipulation of loudness in a MIDI performance.

Resource List

To learn more about MIDI, contact:

The MIDI Manufacturers Association: P.O. Box 3173, La Habra, CA 90632-3173;
http://www.earthlink.net/~mma/

The International MIDI Association: (818)346-8578

Music Hardware Manufacturers:

Casio, Inc.: 570 Mt. Pleasant Avenue, Dover, NJ 07801; (201)361-5400,
http://www.casio-usa.com/

E-MU Systems, Inc. and KAT: 1600 Green Hills Road, P.O. Box 660015, Scotts
Valley, CA 95067; (408)438-1921, http://www.mw3.com/emu/

Korg USA, Inc.: 316 South Service Road, Melville, NY 11747-3201; (516)333-
9100, http://www.korg.com/

Kurzweil Music Systems: 13336 Alondra Boulevard, Cerritos, CA 90703-2245;
(310)926-3200, http://www.youngchang.com/kurzweil/

Mackie Designs: 16220 Wood-Red Road NE, Woodinville, WA 98072;
(206)487-4333

Mark of the Unicorn: 1280 Massachusetts Avenue, Cambridge, MA 02138;
(617)576-2760, http://www.motu.com/

MIDIMan: 45 East Joseph Street, Arcardia, CA 91006; (818)445-7564,
http://www.midifarm.com/midiman/

Opcode Systems, Inc. and Musicquest: 3950 Fabian Way, Suite 100, Palo Alto,
CA 94303; (415)856-3333, http://www.opcode.com/

Roland Corp. U.S.: 7200 Dominion Circle, Los Angeles, CA 90040-3696;
http://www.rolandus.com/

Yamaha Corporation of America: 6600 Orangethorpe Avenue, Buena Park, CA
90620; (714)522-9011, http://www.yamaha.com/

Zeta Music: 2230 Livingston Street, Oakland, CA 94606; (510)261-1702,
http://www.lscn.com/zeta/

Music Software Developers:

Ars Nova: P.O. Box 637, Kirkland, WA 98083; (425)889-0927, http://www.ars-nova.com

Cakewalk: P.O. Box 760, 44 Pleasant St., Watertown, MA 02272; (617)926-2480, www.cakewalk.com

Mark of the Unicorn: 1280 Massachusetts Avenue, Cambridge, MA 02138; (617)576-2760, http://www.motu.com/

Opcode Systems, Inc. and Musicquest: 3950 Fabian Way, Suite 100, Palo Alto, CA 94303; (415)856-3333, http://www.opcode.com/

Passport Designs, Inc.: 1151-D Triton Drive, Foster City, CA 94404; (415)349-6224, http://www.pasportdesigns.com/

PG Music, Inc.: 266 Elmwood Avenue, Suite 111, Buffalo, NY 14222; (905)528-2368, www.islandnet.com/~pgmusic/pgmusic.html

Voyetra Technologies: 5 Odell Plaza, Yonkers, NY 10701; (914)966-0600, http://www.voyetra.com/

Warner Bros. Publications: 15800 NW 48th Avenue, Miami, FL 33014; (305)521-1600

Lee Whitmore

Lee Whitmore, Ed.D., is an educator, musician, technologist and author. He is the Director of SoundTree, the educational division of Korg USA, a leading synthesizer manufacturer. He teaches and presents seminars on the applications of music technology in education throughout the United States, and is a trained pianist and synthesizer player.

An advocate of the benefits of technology in music learning and teaching, Lee has studied the uses of electronic musical instruments and computers for more than a decade. At Columbia University Teachers College Lee recently completed a doctorate in education on the applications of electronic keyboards in music teaching. Lee also served as Teachers College's Instructor of Electronic Music for four years.

Lee is a teacher of teachers, and a developer of music technology products for the home and classroom (with six years experience as a member of Korg's product development team). His experiences have helped him to develop a unique perspective on teaching and learning how to use music technology, and he has a clear and concise way of presenting music technology to new users.

One of Lee's recent graduate students wrote, "Lee is a Zen Master of music technology!" After reading this book you will understand why.